An Old Town By the Sea

by

Thomas Bailey Aldrich

Double9 BOOKS

An Old Town By the Sea

by Thomas Bailey Aldrich

ISBN: 978-93-64289-66-5

Published by

DOUBLE 9 BOOKS
2/13-B, Ansari Road
Daryaganj, New Delhi – 110002
info@double9books.com
www.double9books.com
Tel. 011-40042856

ABOUT THE AUTHOR

Thomas Bailey Aldrich (1836-1907) was an American poet, novelist, and editor, known for his contributions to American literature during the late 19th and early 20th centuries. Born in Portsmouth, New Hampshire, Aldrich began his career as a journalist and published his first book of poetry, "The Bells" and Other Poems, in 1855 at the age of 19. Aldrich's literary style is characterized by its lyrical elegance and romantic sensibility, often reflecting themes of nostalgia, beauty, and the passage of time. He was influenced by both American and European literary traditions, and his work often explored themes of memory, nature, and the human experience. In addition to poetry, Aldrich wrote several novels, including "The Story of a Bad Boy" (1870), which remains one of his most popular works. This semi-autobiographical novel is considered a classic of American literature for its portrayal of childhood and coming-of-age experiences. Aldrich also had a successful career as an editor, working for prominent publications such as "The Atlantic Monthly" and "Harper's Magazine." He was known for his editorial skills and for fostering the careers of other writers of his time. Throughout his life, Aldrich maintained a strong connection to New England, often drawing inspiration from its landscapes and cultural heritage. His poetry and prose continue to be admired for their craftsmanship, evocative imagery, and enduring themes.

Thomas Bailey Aldrich passed away in 1907, leaving behind a legacy of literary achievement that continues to be celebrated in American literature. His works remain an important part of the canon, admired for their lyricism, emotional depth, and insightful reflections on the human condition.

CONTENTS

PISCATAQUA RIVER

Thou singest by the gleaming isles,
By woods, and fields of corn,
Thou singest, and the sunlight smiles
Upon my birthday morn.

But I within a city, I,
So full of vague unrest,
Would almost give my life to lie
An hour upon upon thy breast.

To let the wherry listless go,
And, wrapt in dreamy joy,
Dip, and surge idly to and fro,
Like the red harbor-buoy;

To sit in happy indolence,
To rest upon the oars,
And catch the heavy earthy scents
That blow from summer shores;

To see the rounded sun go down,
And with its parting fires
Light up the windows of the town
And burn the tapering spires;

And then to hear the muffled tolls
From steeples slim and white,
And watch, among the Isles of Shoals,
The Beacon's orange light.

O River! flowing to the main
Through woods, and fields of corn,
Hear thou my longing and my pain
This sunny birthday morn;

And take this song which fancy shapes
To music like thine own,
And sing it to the cliffs and capes
And crags where I am known!

I
CAPTAIN JOHN SMITH

I CALL it an old town, but it is only relatively old. When one reflects on the countless centuries that have gone to the for-mation of this crust of earth on which we temporarily move, the most ancient cities on its surface seem merely things of the week before last. It was only the other day, then—that is to say, in the month of June, 1603—that one Martin Pring, in the ship Speedwell, an enormous ship of nearly fifty tons burden, from Bristol, England, sailed up the Piscataqua River. The Speedwell, numbering thirty men, officers and crew, had for consort the Discoverer, of twenty-six tons and thirteen men. After following the windings of "the brave river" for twelve miles or more, the two vessels turned back and put to sea again, having failed in the chief object of the expedition, which was to obtain a cargo of the medicinal sassafras-tree, from the bark of which, as well known to our ancestors, could be distilled the Elixir of Life.

It was at some point on the left bank of the Piscataqua, three or four miles from the mouth of the river, that worthy Master Pring probably effected one of his several landings. The beautiful stream widens suddenly at this place, and the green banks, then covered with a network of strawberry vines, and sloping invitingly to the lip of the crystal water, must have won the tired mariners.

The explorers found themselves on the edge of a vast forest of oak, hemlock, maple, and pine; but they saw no sassafras-trees to speak of, nor did they encounter—what would have been infinitely less to their taste—and red-men. Here and there were discoverable the scattered ashes of fires where the Indians had encamped earlier in the spring; they were absent now, at the silvery falls, higher up the stream, where fish abounded at that season. The soft June breeze, laden with the delicate breath of wild-flowers and the pungent odors of spruce and pine, ruffled the duplicate sky in the water; the new leaves lisped pleasantly in the tree tops, and the birds were singing as if they had gone mad. No ruder sound or movement of life disturbed the primeval solitude. Master Pring would scarcely recognize the spot were he to land there to-day.

Eleven years afterwards a much cleverer man than the commander of the Speedwell dropped anchor in the Piscataqua—Captain John Smith of famous memory. After slaying Turks in hand-to-hand combats, and doing all sorts of doughty deeds wherever he chanced to decorate the globe with his presence, he had come with two vessels to the fisheries on the rocky selvage of Maine, when curiosity, or perhaps a deeper motive, led him to examine the neighboring shore lines. With eight of his men in a small boat, a ship's yawl, he skirted the coast from Penobscot Bay to Cape Cod, keeping his eye open. This keeping his eye open was a peculiarity of the little captain; possibly a family trait. It was Smith who really discovered the Isles of Shoals, exploring in person those masses of bleached rock—those "isles assez hautes," of which the French navigator Pierre de Guast, Sieur de Monts, had caught a bird's-eye glimpse through the twilight in 1605. Captain Smith christened the group Smith's Isles, a title which posterity, with singular persistence of ingratitude, has ignored. It was a tardy sense of justice that expressed itself a few years ago in erecting on Star Island a simple marble shaft to the memory of JOHN SMITH—the multitudinous! Perhaps this long delay is explained by a natural hesitation to label a monument so ambiguously.

The modern Jason, meanwhile, was not without honor in his own country, whatever may have happened to him in his own house, for the poet George Wither addressed a copy of pompous verses "To his Friend Captain Smith, upon his Description of New England." "Sir," he says—

"Sir: your Relations I haue read: which shew

Ther's reason I should honor them and you:

And if their meaning I have vnderstood,

I dare to censure thus: Your Project's good;

And may (if follow'd) doubtlesse quit the paine

With honour, pleasure and a trebble gaine;

Beside the benefit that shall arise

To make more happy our Posterities."

The earliest map of this portion of our seaboard was prepared by Smith and laid before Prince Charles, who asked to give the country a name. He christened it New England. In that remarkable map the site of Portsmouth is call Hull, and Kittery and York are known as Boston.

It was doubtless owing to Captain John Smith's representation on his return to England that the Laconia Company selected the banks of the Piscataqua for their plantation. Smith was on an intimate footing with Sir Ferinand Gorges, who, five years subsequently, made a tour of inspection along the New England coast, in company with John Mason, then Governor of Newfoundland. One of the results of this summer cruise is the town of Portsmouth, among whose leafy ways, and into some of whose old-fashioned houses, I purpose to take the reader, if he have an idle hour on his hands. Should we meet the flitting ghost of some old-time worthy, on the staircase or at a lonely street corner, the reader must be prepared for it.

II
ALONG THE WATER SIDE

IT is not supposable that the early settlers selected the site of their plantation on account of its picturesqueness. They were influenced entirely by the lay of the land, its nearness and easy access to the sea, and the secure harbor it offered to their fishing-vessels; yet they could not have chosen a more beautiful spot had beauty been the sole consideration. The first settlement was made at Odiorne's Point—the Pilgrims' Rock of New Hampshire; there the Manor, or Mason's Hall, was built by the Laconia Company in 1623. It was not until 1631 that the Great House was erected by Humphrey Chadborn on Strawberry Bank. Mr. Chadborn, consciously or unconsciously, sowed a seed from which a city has sprung.

The town of Portsmouth stretches along the south bank of the Piscataqua, about two miles from the sea as the crow flies—three miles following the serpentine course of the river. The stream broadens suddenly at this point, and at flood tide, lying without a ripple in a basin formed by the interlocked islands and the mainland, it looks more like an island lake than a river. To the unaccustomed eye there is no visible outlet. Standing on one of the wharves at the foot of State Street or Court Street, a stranger would at first scarcely suspect the contiguity of the ocean. A little observation, however, would show him that he was in a seaport. The rich red rust on the gables and roofs of ancient buildings looking seaward would tell him that. There is a fitful saline flavor in the air, and if while he gazed a dense white fog should come rolling in, like a line of phantom breakers, he would no longer have any doubts.

It is of course the oldest part of the town that skirts the river, though few of the notable houses that remain are to be found there. Like all New England settlements, Portsmouth was built of wood, and has been subjected to extensive conflagrations. You rarely come across a brick building that is not shockingly modern. The first house of the kind was erected by Richard Wibird towards the close of the seventeenth century.

Though many of the old landmarks have been swept away by the fateful hand of time and fire, the town impresses you as a very old town, especially as you saunter along the streets down by the river. The worm-eaten wharves, some of them covered by a sparse, unhealthy beard of grass, and the weather-stained, unoccupied warehouses are sufficient to satisfy a moderate appetite for antiquity. These deserted piers and these long rows of empty barracks, with their sarcastic cranes projecting from the eaves, rather puzzle the stranger. Why this great preparation for a commercial activity that does not exist, and evidently had not for years existed? There are no ships lying at the pier-heads; there are no gangs of stevedores staggering under the heavy cases of merchandise; here and there is a barge laden down to the bulwarks with coal, and here and there a square-rigged schooner from Maine smothered with fragrant planks and clapboards; an imported citizen is fishing at the end of the wharf, a ruminative freckled son of Drogheda, in perfect sympathy with the indolent sunshine that seems to be sole proprietor of these crumbling piles and ridiculous warehouses, from which even the ghost of prosperity has flown.

Once upon a time, however, Portsmouth carried on an extensive trade with the West Indies, threatening as a maritime port to eclipse both Boston and New York. At the windows of these musty counting-rooms which overlook the river near Spring Market used to stand portly merchants, in knee breeches and silver shoe-buckles and plum-colored coats with ruffles at the wrist, waiting for their ships to come up the Narrows; the cries of stevedores and the chants of sailors at the windlass used to echo along the shore where all is silence now. For reasons not worth setting forth, the trade with the Indies abruptly closed, having ruined as well as enriched many a Portsmouth adventurer. This explains the empty warehouses and the unused wharves. Portsmouth remains the interesting widow of a once very lively commerce. I fancy that few fortunes are either made or lost in Portsmouth nowadays. Formerly it turned out the best ships, as it did the ablest ship captains, in the world. There were families in which the love for blue water was in immemorial trait. The boys were always sailors; "a grey-headed shipmaster, in each generation, retiring from the quarter-deck to the homestead, while a boy of fourteen took the hereditary place before the mast, confronting the salt spray and the gale, which had blasted against his sire and grandsire." (1. Hawthorne in his introduction to The Scarlet Letter.) With thousands of miles of sea-line and a score or two of the finest harbors on the globe, we have adroitly turned over our carrying trade to foreign nations.

In other days, as I have said, a high maritime spirit was characteristic of Portsmouth. The town did a profitable business in the war of 1812, sending out a large fleet of the sauciest small craft on record. A pleasant story is told of one of these little privateers—the Harlequin, owned and commanded by

Captain Elihu Brown. The Harlequin one day gave chase to a large ship, which did not seem to have much fight aboard, and had got it into close quarters, when suddenly the shy stranger threw open her ports, and proved to be His Majesty's Ship-of-War Bulwark, seventy-four guns. Poor Captain Brown!

Portsmouth has several large cotton factories and one or two corpulent breweries; it is a wealthy old town, with a liking for first mortgage bonds; but its warmest lover will not claim for it the distinction of being a great mercantile centre. The majority of her young men are forced to seek other fields to reap, and almost every city in the Union, and many a city across the sea, can point to some eminent merchant, lawyer, or what not, as "a Portsmouth boy." Portsmouth even furnished the late king of the Sandwich Islands, Kekuanaoa, with a prime minister, and his nankeen Majesty never had a better. The affection which all these exiles cherish for their birthplace is worthy of remark. On two occasions—in 1852 and 1873, the two hundred and fiftieth anniversary of the settlement of Strawberry Bank—the transplanted sons of Portsmouth were seized with an impulse to return home. Simultaneously and almost without concerted action, the lines of pilgrims took up their march from every quarter of the globe, and swept down with music and banners on the motherly old town.

To come back to the wharves. I do not know of any spot with such a fascinating air of dreams and idleness about it as the old wharf at the end of Court Street. The very fact that it was once a noisy, busy place, crowded with sailors and soldiers—in the war of 1812—gives an emphasis to the quiet that broods over it to-day. The lounger who sits of a summer afternoon on a rusty anchor fluke in the shadow of one of the silent warehouses, and look on the lonely river as it goes murmuring past the town, cannot be too grateful to the India trade for having taken itself off elsewhere.

What a slumberous, delightful, lazy place it is! The sunshine seems to lie a foot deep on the planks of the dusty wharf, which yields up to the warmth a vague perfume of the cargoes of rum, molasses, and spice that used to be piled upon it. The river is as blue as the inside of a harebell. The opposite shore, in the strangely shifting magic lights of sky and water, stretches along like the silvery coast of fairyland. Directly opposite you is the navy yard, and its neat officers' quarters and workshops and arsenals, and its vast shiphouses, in which the keel of many a famous frigate has been laid. Those monster buildings on the water's edge, with their roofs pierced with innumerable little windows, which blink like eyes in the sunlight, and the shiphouses. On your right lies a cluster of small islands,—there are a dozen or more in the harbor—on the most extensive of which you see the fading-away remains of some earthworks thrown up in 1812. Between this—Trefethren's Island—and Peirce's Island lie the Narrows. Perhaps a bark or a sloop-of-war is making up to town; the hulk is hidden amoung the islands, and the topmasts have the effect of sweeping across the dry land. On your left is a long bridge, more than a quarter of a mile in length, set upon piles where the water is twenty or thirty feet deep, leading to the navy yard and Kittery—the Kittery so often the theme of Whittier's verse.

This is a mere outline of the landscape that spreads before you. Its changeful beauty of form and color, with the summer clouds floating over it, is not to be painted in words. I know of many a place where the scenery is more varied and striking; but there is a mandragora quality in the atmosphere here that holds you to the spot, and makes the half-hours seem like minutes. I could fancy a man sitting on the end of that old wharf very contentedly for two or three years, provided it could be always in June.

Perhaps, too, one would desire it to be always high water. The tide falls from eight to twelve feet, and when the water makes out between the wharves some of the picturesqueness makes out also. A corroded section of stovepipe mailed in barnacles, or the skeleton of a hoopskirt protruding from the tide mud like the remains of some old-time wreck, is apt to break the enchantment.

I fear I have given the reader an exaggerated idea of the solitude that reigns along the river-side. Sometimes there is society here of an unconventional kind, if you care to seek it. Aside from the foreign gentleman before mentioned, you are likely to encounter, farther down the shore toward the Point of Graves (a burial-place of the colonial period), a battered and aged native fisherman boiling lobsters on a little gravelly bench, where the river whispers and lisps among the pebbles as the tide creeps in. It is a weather-beaten ex-skipper or ex-pilot, with strands of coarse hair, like seaweed, falling about a face that has the expression of a half-open clam. He is always ready to talk with you, this amphibious person; and if he is not the most entertaining of gossips—more weather-wise that Old Probabilities, and as full of moving incident as Othello himself—then he is not the wintery-haired shipman I used to see a few years ago on the strip of beach just beyond Liberty Bridge, building his drift-wood fire under a great tin boiler, and making it lively for a lot of reluctant lobsters.

I imagine that very little change has taken place in this immediate locality, known prosaically as Puddle Dock, during the past fifty or sixty years. The view you get looking across Liberty Bridge, Water Street, is probably the same in every respect that presented itself to the eyes of the town folk a century ago. The flagstaff, on the right, is the representative of the old "standard of liberty" which the Sons planted on this spot in January,

1766, signalizing their opposition to the enforcement of the Stamp Act. On the same occasion the patriots called at the house of Mr. George Meserve, the agent for distributing the stamps in New Hampshire, and relieved him of his stamp-master's commission, which document they carried on the point of a sword through the town to Liberty Bridge (the Swing Bridge), where they erected the staff, with the motto, "Liberty, Property, and no Stamp!"

The Stamp Act was to go into operation on the first day of November. On the previous morning the "New Hampshire Gazette" appeared with a deep black border and all the typographical emblems of affliction, for was not Liberty dead? At all events, the "Gazette" itself was as good as dead, since the printer could no longer publish it if he were to be handicapped by a heavy tax. "The day was ushered in by the tolling of all the bells in town, the vessels in the harbor had their colors hoisted half-mast high; about three o'clock a funeral procession was formed, having a coffin with this inscription, LIBERTY, AGED 145, STAMPT. It moved from the state house, with two unbraced drums, through the principal streets. As it passed the Parade, minute-guns were fired; at the place of interment a speech was delivered on the occasion, stating the many advantages we had received and the melancholy prospect before us, at the seeming departure of our invaluable liberties. But some sign of life appearing, Liberty was not deposited in the grave; it was rescued by a number of her sons, the motto changed to Liberty revived, and carried off in triumph. The detestable Act was buried in its stead, and the clods of the valley were laid upon it; the bells changed their melancholy sound to a more joyful tone." (1. Annals of Portsmouth, by Nathaniel Adams, 1825.)

With this side glance at one of the curious humors of the time, we resume our peregrinations.

Turning down a lane on your left, a few rods beyond Liberty Bridge, you reach a spot known as the Point of Graves, chiefly interesting as showing what a graveyard may come to if it last long enough. In 1671 one Captain John Pickering, of whom we shall have more to say, ceded to the town a piece of ground on this neck for burial purposes. It is an odd-shaped lot, comprising about half an acre, inclosed by a crumbling red brick wall two or three feet high, with wood capping. The place is overgrown with thistles, rank grass, and fungi; the black slate headstones have mostly fallen over; those that still make a pretense of standing slant to every point of the compass, and look as if they were being blown this way and that by a mysterious gale which leaves everything else untouched; the mounds have sunk to the common level, and the old underground tombs have collapsed.

Here and there the moss and weeds you can pick out some name that shines in the history of the early settlement; hundreds of the flower of the colony lie here, but the known and the unknown, gentle and simple, mingle their dust on a perfect equality now. The marble that once bore a haughty coat of arms is as smooth as the humblest slate stone guiltless of heraldry. The lion and the unicorn, wherever they appear on some cracked slab, are very much tamed by time. The once fat-faced cherubs, with wing at either cheek, are the merest skeletons now. Pride, pomp, grief, and remembrance are all at end. No reverent feet come here, no tears fall here; the old graveyard itself is dead! A more dismal, uncanny spot than this at twilight would be hard to find. It is noticed that when the boys pass it after nightfall, they always go by whistling with a gayety that is perfectly hollow.

Let us get into some cheerfuler neighborhood!

III
A STROLL ABOUT TOWN

AS you leave the river front behind you, and pass "up town," the streets grow wider, and the architecture becomes more ambitious—streets fringed with beautiful old trees and lined with commodious private dwellings, mostly square white houses, with spacious halls running through the centre. Previous to the Revolution, white paint was seldom used on houses, and the diamond-shaped window pane was almost universal. Many of the residences stand back from the brick or flagstone sidewalk, and have pretty gardens at the side or in the rear, made bright with dahlias and sweet with cinnamon roses. If you chance to live in a town where the authorities cannot rest until they have destroyed every precious tree within their blighting reach, you will be especially charmed by the beauty of the streets of Portsmouth. In some parts of the town, when the chestnuts are in blossom, you would fancy yourself in a garden in fairyland. In spring, summer, and autumn the foliage is the glory of the fair town—her luxuriant green and golden treeses! Nothing could seem more like the work of enchantment than the spectacle which certain streets in Portsmouth present in the midwinter after a heavy snowstorm. You may walk for miles under wonderful silvery arches formed by the overhanging and interlaced boughs of the trees, festooned with a drapery even more graceful and dazzling than springtime gives them. The numerous elms and maples which shade the principal thoroughfares are not the result of chance, but the ample reward of the loving care that is taken to preserve the trees. There is a society in Portsmouth devoted to arboriculture. It is not unusual there for persons to leave legacies to be expended in setting out shade and ornamental trees along some favorite walk. Richards Avenue, a long, unbuilt thoroughfare leading from Middle Street to the South Burying-Ground, perpetuates the name of a citizen who gave the labor of his own hands to the beautifying of that windswept and barren road the cemetery. This fondness and care for trees seems to be a matter of heredity. So far back as 1660 the selectmen instituted a fine of five shillings for the cutting of timber or any other wood from off the town common, excepting under special conditions.

In the business section of the town trees are few. The chief business streets are Congress and Market. Market Street is the stronghold of the dry-goods shops. There are seasons, I suppose, when these shops are crowded, but I have never happened to be in Portsmouth at the time. I seldom pass through the narrow cobble-paved street without wondering where the customers are that must keep all these flourishing little establishments going. Congress Street—a more elegant thoroughfare than Market—is the Nevski Prospekt of Portsmouth. Among the prominent buildings is the Athenaeum, containing a reading-room and library. From the high roof of this building the stroller will do well to take a glance at the surrounding country. He will naturally turn seaward for the more picturesque aspects. If the day is clear, he will see the famous Isle of Shoals, lying nine miles away—Appledore, Smutty-Nose, Star Island, White Island, etc.; there are nine of them in all. On Appledore is Laighton's Hotel, and near it the summer cottage of Celia Thaxter, the poet of the Isles. On the northern end of Star Island is the quaint town of Gosport, with a tiny stone church perched like a sea-gull on its highest rock. A mile southwest form Star Island lies White Island, on which is a lighthouse. Mrs. Thaxter calls this the most picturesque of the group. Perilous neighbors, O mariner! in any but the serenest weather, these wrinkled, scarred, are storm-smitten rocks, flanked by wicked sunken ledges that grow white at the lip with rage when the great winds blow!

How peaceful it all looks off there, on the smooth emerald sea! and how softly the waves seem to break on yonder point where the unfinished fort is! That is the ancient town of Newcastle, to reach which from Portsmouth you have to cross three bridges with the most enchanting scenery in New Hampshire lying on either hand. At Newcastle the poet Stedman has built for his summerings an enviable little stone chateau—a seashell into which I fancy the sirens creep to warm themselves during the winter months. So it is never without its singer.

Opposite Newcastle is Kittery Point, a romantic spot, where Sir William Pepperell, the first American baronet, once lived, and where his tomb now is, in his orchard across the road, a few hundred yards from the "goodly mansion" he built. The knight's tomb and the old Pepperell House, which has been somewhat curtailed of it fair proportions, are the objects of frequent pilgrimages to Kittery Point.

From the elevation (the roof of the Athenaeun) the navy yard, the river with its bridges and islands, the clustered gables of Kittery and Newcastle, the illimitable ocean beyond make a picture worth climbing four or five flights of stairs to gaze upon. Glancing down on the town nestled in the foliage, it seems like a town dropped by chance in the midst of a forest. Among the prominent objects which lift themselves above the tree tops are the belfries of the various churches, the white façade of the custom house, and the mansard and chimneys of the Rockingham, the principal hotel. The pilgrim will be surprised to find in Portsmouth one of the most completely appointed hotels in the United States. The antiquarian may lament the demolition of the old Bell Tavern, and think regretfully of the good cheer once furnished the wayfarer by Master Stavers at the sign of the Earl of Halifax, and by Master Stoodley at his inn on Daniel Street; but the ordinary traveler will thank his stars, and confess that his lines have fallen in pleasant places, when he finds himself among the frescoes of the Rockingham.

Obliquely opposite the doorstep of the Athenaeum—we are supposed to be on terra firma again—stands the Old North Church, a substantial wooden building, handsomely set on what is called The Parade, a large open space formed by the junction of Congress, Market, Daniel, and Pleasant streets. Here in days innocent of water-works stood the town pump, which on more than one occasion served as whipping-post.

The churches of Portsmouth are more remarkable for their number than their architecture. With the exception of the Stone Church they are constructed of wood or plain brick in the simplest style. St. John's Church is the only one likely to attract the eye of a stranger. It is finely situated on the crest of Church Hill, overlooking the ever-beautiful river. The present edifice was built in 1808 on the site of what was known as Queen's Chapel, erected in 1732, and destroyed by fire December 24, 1806. The chapel was named in honor of Queen Caroline, who furnished the books for the altar and pulpit, the plate, and two solid mahogany chairs, which are still in use in St. John's. Within the chancel rail is a curious font of porphyry, taken by Colonel John Tufton Mason at the capture of Senegal from the French in 1758, and presented to the Episcopal Society on 1761. The peculiarly sweet-toned bell which calls the parishioners of St. John's together every Sabbath is, I believe, the same that formerly hung in the belfry of the old Queen's Chapel. If so, the bell has a history of its own. It was brought from Louisburg at the time of the reduction of that place in 1745, and given to the church by the officers of the New Hampshire troops.

The Old South Meeting-House is not to be passed without mention. It is among the most aged survivals of pre-revolutionary days. Neither its architecture not its age, however, is its chief warrant for our notice. The absurd number of windows in this battered old structure is what strikes the passer-by. The church was erected by subscription, and these closely set large windows are due to Henry Sherburne, one of the wealthiest citizens of the period, who agreed to pay for whatever glass was used. If the building could have been composed entirely of glass it would have been done by the thrifty parishioners.

Portsmouth is rich in graveyards—they seem to be a New England specialty—ancient and modern. Among the old burial-places the one attached to St. John's Church is perhaps the most interesting. It has not been permitted to fall into ruin, like the old cemetery at the Point of Graves. When a headstone here topples over it is kindly lifted up and set on its pins again, and encouraged to do its duty. If it utterly refuses, and is not shamming decrepitude, it has its face sponged, and is allowed to rest and sun itself against the wall of the church with a row of other exempts. The trees are kept pruned, the grass trimmed, and here and there is a rosebush drooping with a weight of pensive pale roses, as becomes a rosebush in a churchyard.

The place has about it an indescribable soothing atmosphere of respectability and comfort. Here rest the remains of the principal and loftiest in rank in their generation of the citizens of Portsmouth prior to the Revolution—stanch, royalty-loving governors, counselors, and secretaries of the Providence of New Hampshire, all snugly gathered under the motherly wing of the Church of England. It is almost impossible to walk anywhere without stepping on a governor. You grow haughty in spirit after a while, and scorn to tread on anything less than one of His Majesty's colonels or secretary under the Crown. Here are the tombs of the Atkinsons, the Jaffreys, the Sherburnes, the Sheafes, the Marshes, the Mannings, the Gardners, and others of the quality. All around you underfoot are tumbled-in coffins, with here and there a rusty sword atop, and faded escutcheons, and crumbling armorial devices. You are moving in the very best society.

This, however, is not the earliest cemetery in Portsmouth. An hour's walk from the Episcopal yard will bring you to the spot, already mentioned, where the first house was built and the first grave made, at Odiorne's Point. The exact site of the Manor is not known, but it is supposed to be a few rods north of an old well of still-flowing water, at which the Tomsons and the Hiltons and their comrades slaked their thirst more than two hundred and sixty years ago. Oriorne's Point is owned by Mr. Eben L. Odiorne, a lineal descendant of the worthy who held the property in 1657. Not far from the old spring is the resting-place of the earliest pioneers.

"This first cemetery of the white man in New Hampshire," writes Mr. Brewster, (1. Mr. Charles W. Brewster, for nearly fifty years the editor of the Portsmouth Journal, and the author of two volumes of local sketches to which the writer of these pages here acknowledges his indebtedness.) "occupies a space of perhaps one hundred feet by ninety, and is well walled in. The western side is now used as a burial-place for the family, but two thirds of it is filled with perhaps forty graves, indicated by rough head and foot stones. Who there rest no one now living knows. But the same care is taken of their quiet beds as if they were of the proprietor's own family. In 1631 Mason sent over about eighty emigrants many of whom died in a few years, and here they were probably buried. Here too, doubtless, rest the remains of several of those whose names stand conspicuous in our early state records."

IV
A STROLL ABOUT TOWN (continued)

WHEN Washington visited Portsmouth in 1789 he was not much impressed by the architecture of the little town that had stood by him so stoutly in the struggle for independence. "There are some good houses," he writes, in a diary kept that year during a tour through Connecticut, Massachusetts, and New Hampshire, "among which Colonel Langdon's may be esteemed the first; but in general they are indifferent, and almost entirely of wood. On wondering at this, as the country is full of stone and good clay for bricks, I was told that on account of the fogs and damp they deemed them wholesomer, and for that reason preferred wood buildings."

The house of Colonel Langdon, on Pleasant Street, is an excellent sample of the solid and dignified abodes which our great-grandsires had the sense to build. The art of their construction seems to have been a lost art these fifty years. Here Governor John Langdon resided from 1782 until the time of his death in 1819—a period during which many an illustrious man passed between those two white pillars that support the little balcony over the front door; among the rest Louis Philippe and his brothers, the Ducs de Montpensier and Beaujolais, and the Marquis de Chastellus, a major-general in the French army, serving under the Count de Rochambeau, whom he accompanied from France to the States in 1780. The journal of the marquis contains this reference to his host: "After dinner we went to drink tea with Mr. Langdon. He is a handsome man, and of noble carriage; he has been a member of Congress, and is now one of the first people of the country; his house is elegant and well furnished, and the apartments admirably well wainscoted" (this reads like Mr. Samuel Pepys); "and he has a good manuscript chart of the harbor of Portsmouth. Mrs. Langdon, his wife, is young, fair, and tolerably handsome, but I conversed less with her than her husband, in whose favor I was prejudiced from knowing that he had displayed great courage and patriotism at the time of Burgoynes's expedition."

It was at the height of the French Revolution that the three sons of the Due d'Orleans were entertained at the Langdon mansion. Years afterward, when

Louis Philippe was on the throne of France, he inquired of a Portsmouth lady presented at his court if the mansion of ce brave Gouverneur Langdon was still in existence.

The house stands back a decorous distance from the street, under the shadows of some gigantic oaks or elms, and presents an imposing appearance as you approach it over the tessellated marble walk. A hundred or two feet on either side of the gate, and abutting on the street, is a small square building of brick, one story in height—probably the porter's lodge and tool-house of former days. There is a large fruit garden attached to the house, which is in excellent condition, taking life comfortably, and having the complacent air of a well-preserved beau of the ancien regime. The Langdon mansion was owned and long occupied by the late Rev. Dr. Burroughs, for a period of forty-seven years the esteemed rector or St. John's Church.

At the other end of Pleasant Street is another notable house, to which we shall come by and by. Though President Washington found Portsmouth but moderately attractive from an architectural point of view, the visitor of to-day, if he have an antiquarian taste, will find himself embarrassed by the number of localities and buildings that appeal to his interest. Many of these buildings were new and undoubtedly commonplace enough at the date of Washington's visit; time and association have given them a quaintness and a significance which now make their architecture a question of secondary importance.

One might spend a fortnight in Portsmouth exploring the nooks and corners over which history has thrown a charm, and by no means exhaust the list. I cannot do more than attempt to describe—and that very briefly—a few of the typical old houses. On this same Pleasant Street there are several which we must leave unnoted, with their spacious halls and carven staircases, their antiquated furniture and old silver tankards and choice Copleys. Numerous examples of this artist's best manner are to be found here. To live in Portsmouth without possessing a family portrait done by Copley is like living in Boston without having an ancestor in the old Granary Burying-Ground. You can exist, but you cannot be said to flourish. To make this statement smooth, I will remark that every one in Portsmouth has a Copley—or would have if a fair division were made.

In the better sections of the town the houses are kept in such excellent repair, and have so smart an appearance with their bright green blinds and freshly painted woodwork, that you are likely to pass many an old landmark without suspecting it. Whenever you see a house with a gambrel roof, you may be almost positive that the house is at least a hundred years old, for the gambrel roof went out of fashion after the Revolution.

On the corner of Daniel and Chapel streets stands the oldest brick building in Portsmouth—the Warner House. It was built in 1718 by Captain Archibald Macpheadris, a Scotchman, as his name indicates, a wealthy merchant, and a member of the King's Council. He was the chief projector of one of the earliest iron-works established in America. Captain Macpheadris married Sarah Wentworth, one of the sixteen children of Governor John Wentworth, and died in 1729, leaving a daughter, Mary, whose portrait, with that of her mother, painted by the ubiquitous Copley, still hangs in the parlor of this house, which is not known by the name of Captain Macpheadris, but by that of his son-in-law, Hon. Jonathan Warner, a member of the King's Council until the revolt of the colonies. "We well recollect Mr. Warner," says Mr. Brewster, writing in 1858, "as one of the last of the cocked hats. As in a vision of early childhood he is still before us, in all the dignity of the aristocratic crown officers. That broad-backed, long-skirted brown coat, those small-clothes and silk stockings, those silver buckles, and that cane—we see them still, although the life that filled and moved them ceased half a century ago."

The Warner House, a three-story building with gambrel roof and luthern windows, is as fine and substantial an exponent of the architecture of the period as you are likely to meet with anywhere in New England. The eighteen-inch walls are of brick brought from Holland, as were also many of the materials used in the building—the hearth-stones, tiles, etc. Hewn-stone underpinnings were seldom adopted in those days; the brick-work rests directly upon the solid walls of the cellar. The interior is rich in paneling and wood carvings about the mantel-shelves, the deep-set windows, and along the cornices. The halls are wide and long, after a by-gone fashion, with handsome staircases, set at an easy angle, and not standing nearly upright, like those ladders by which one reaches the upper chambers of a modern house. The principal rooms are paneled to the ceiling, and have large open chimney-places, adorned with the quaintest of Dutch files. In one of the parlors of the Warner House there is a choice store of family relics—china, silver-plate, costumes, old clocks, and the like. There are some interesting paintings, too—not by Copley this time. On a broad space each side of the hall windows, at the head of the staircase, are pictures of two Indians, life size. They are probably portraits of some of the numerous chiefs with whom Captain Macphaedris had dealings, for the captain was engaged in the fur as well as in the iron business. Some enormous elk antlers, presented to Macpheadris by his red friends, are hanging in the lower hall.

By mere chance, thirty or forty years ago, some long-hidden paintings on the walls of this lower hall were brought to light. In repairing the front entry it became necessary to remove the paper, of which four or five layers had accumulated. A one place, where several coats had peeled off cleanly, a horse's hoof was observed by a little girl of the family. The workman then began removing the paper carefully; first the legs, then the body of a horse with a rider were revealed, and the astonished paper-hanger presently stood before a life-size representation of Governor Phipps on his charger. The workman called other persons to his assistance, and the remaining portions of the wall were speedily stripped, laying bare four or five hundred square feet covered with sketches in color, landscapes, views of unknown cities, Biblical scenes, and modern figure-pieces, among which was a lady at a spinning-wheel. Until then no person in the land of the living had had any knowledge of those hidden pictures. An old dame of eighty, who had visited at the house intimately ever since her childhood, all but refused to believe her spectacles (though Supply Ham made them(1.)) when brought face to face with the frescoes. (1. In the early part of this century, Supply Ham was the leading optician and watchmaker of Portsmouth.)

The place is rich in bricabrac, but there is nothing more curious that these incongruous printings, clearly the work of a practiced hand. Even the outside of the old edifice is not without its interest for an antiquarian. The lightening-rod which protects the Warner House to-day was put up under Benjamin Franklin's own supervision in 1762—such at all events is the credited tradition—and is supposed to be the first rod put up in New Hampshire. A lightening-rod "personally conducted" by Benjamin Franklin ought to be an attractive object to even the least susceptible electricity. The Warner House has another imperative claim on the good-will of the visitor—it is not positively known that George Washington ever slept there.

The same assertion cannot be made on connection with the old yellow barracks situated in the southwest corner of Court and Atkinson streets. Famous old houses seem to have an intuitive perception of the value of corner lots. If it is a possible thing, they always set themselves down on the most desirable spots. It is beyond a doubt that Washington slept not only one night, but several nights, under this roof; for this was a celebrated tavern previous and subsequent to the War of Independence, and Washington made it his headquarters during his visit to Portsmouth in 1797. When I was a boy I knew an old lady—not one of the preposterous old ladies in the newspapers, who have all their faculties unimpaired, but a real old lady, whose ninety-nine years were beginning to tell on her—who had known Washington very well. She was a girl in her teens when he came to Portsmouth. The President was the staple of her conversation during the last ten years of her life, which she passed in the Stavers House, bedridden; and I think those ten years were in a manner rendered short and pleasant to the old gentlewoman by the memory of a compliment to her complexion which Washington probably never paid to it.

The old hotel—now a very unsavory tenement-house—was built by John Tavers, innkeeper, in 1770, who planted in front of the door a tall post, from which swung the sign of the Earl of Halifax. Stavers had previously kept an inn of the same name on Queen, now State Street.

It is a square three-story building, shabby and dejected, giving no hint of the really important historical associations that cluster about it. At the time of its erection it was no doubt considered a rather grand structure, for buildings of three stories were rare in Portsmouth. Even in 1798, of the six hundred and twenty-six dwelling houses of which the town boasted, eighty-six were of one story, five hundred and twenty-four were of two stories, and only sixteen of three stories. The Stavers inn has the regulation gambrel roof, but is lacking in those wood ornaments which are usually seen over the doors and windows of the more prominent houses of that epoch. It was, however, the hotel of the period.

That same worn doorstep upon which Mr. O'Shaughnessy now stretches himself of a summer afternoon, with a short clay pipe stuck between his lips, and his hat crushed down on his brows, revolving the sad vicissitude of things—that same doorstep has been pressed by the feet of generals and marquises and grave dignitaries upon whom depended the destiny of the States—officers in gold lace and scarlet cloth, and high-heeled belles in patch, powder, and paduasoy. At this door the Flying Stage Coach, which crept from Boston, once a week set down its load of passengers—and distinguished passengers they often were. Most of the chief celebrities of the land, before and after the secession of the colonies, were the guests of Master Stavers, at the sign of the Earl of Halifax.

While the storm was brewing between the colonies and the mother country, it was in a back room of the tavern that the adherents of the crown met to discuss matters. The landlord himself was a amateur loyalist, and when the full cloud was on the eve of breaking he had an early intimation of the coming tornado. The Sons of Liberty had long watched with sullen eyes the secret sessions of the Tories in Master Stavers's tavern, and one morning the patriots quietly began cutting down the post which supported the obnoxious emblem. Mr. Stavers, who seems not to have been belligerent himself, but the cause of belligerence in others, sent out his black slave with orders to stop proceedings. The negro, who was armed with an axe, struck but a single blow and disappeared. This blow fell upon the head of Mark Noble; it did not kill him, but left him an insane man till the day of his death, forty years afterward. A furious mob at once collected, and made an attack on the tavern, bursting in the doors and shattering every pane of glass in the windows. It was only through the intervention of Captain John Langdon, a warm and popular patriot, that the hotel was saved from destruction.

In the mean while Master Stavers had escaped through the stables in the rear. He fled to Stratham, where he was given refuge by his friend William Pottle, a most appropriately named gentleman, who had supplied the hotel with ale. The excitement blew over after a time, and Stavers was induced to return to Portsmouth. He was seized by the Committee of Safety, and lodged in Exeter jail, when his loyalty, which had really never been very high, went down below zero; he took the oath of allegiance, and shortly after his released reopened the hotel. The honest face of William Pitt appeared on the repentant sign, vice Earl of Halifax, ignominiously removed, and Stavers was himself again. In the state records is the following letter from poor Noble begging for the enlargement of John Stavers:—

PORTSMOUTH, February 3, 1777. To the Committee of Safety of the Town of Exeter: GENTLEMEN,—As I am informed that Mr. Stivers is in confinement in gaol upon my account contrary to my desire, for when I was at Mr. Stivers a fast day I had no ill nor ment none against the Gentleman but by bad luck or misfortune I have received a bad Blow but it is so well that I hope to go out in a day or two. So by this gentlemen of the Committee I hope you will release the gentleman upon my account. I am yours to serve. MARK NOBLE, A friend to my country.

From that period until I know not what year the Stavers House prospered. It was at the sign of the William Pitt that the officers of the French fleet boarded in 1782, and hither came the Marquis Lafayette, all the way from Providence, to visit them. John Hancock, Elbridge Gerry, Rutledge, and other signers of the Declaration sojourned here at various times. It was here General Knox—"that stalwart man, two officers in size and three in lungs"—was wont to order his dinner, and in a stentorian voice compliment Master Stavers on the excellence of his larder. One day—it was at the time of the French Revolution—Louis Philippe and his two brothers applied at the door of the William Pitt for lodgings; but the tavern was full, and the future king, with his companions, found comfortable quarters under the hospitable roof of Governor Langdon in Pleasant Street.

A record of the scenes, tragic and humorous, that have been enacted within this old yellow house on the corner would fill a volume. A vivid picture of the social and public life of the old time might be painted by a skillful hand, using the two Earl of Halifax inns for a background. The painter would find gay and sombre pigments ready mixed for his palette, and a hundred romantic incidents waiting for his canvas. One of these romantic episodes has been turned to very pretty account by Longfellow in the last series of The Tales of a Wayside Inn—the marriage of Governor Benning Wentworth with Martha Hilton, a sort of second edition of King Cophetua and the Beggar Maid.

Martha Hilton was a poor girl, whose bare feet and ankles and scant drapery when she was a child, and even after she was well in the bloom of her teens, used to scandalize good Dame Stavers, the innkeeper's wife. Standing one afternoon in the doorway of the Earl of Halifax, (1. The first of the two hotels bearing that title. Mr. Brewster commits a slight anachronism in locating the scene of this incident in Jaffrey Street, now Court. The Stavers House was not built until the year of Governor Benning Wentworth's death. Mr. Longfellow, in the poem, does not fall into the same error.

"One hundred years ago, and something more,
In Queen Street, Portsmouth, at her tavern door,
Neat as a pin, and blooming as a rose,
Stood Mistress Stavers in her furbelows.")

Dame Stavers took occasion to remonstrate with the sleek-limbed and lightly draped Martha, who chanced to be passing the tavern, carrying a pail of water, in which, as the poet neatly says, "the shifting sunbeam danced."

"You Pat! you Pat!" cried Mrs. Stavers severely; "why do you go looking so? You should be ashamed to be seen in the street."

"Never mind how I look," says Miss Martha, with a merry laugh, letting slip a saucy brown shoulder out of her dress; "I shall ride in my chariot yet, ma'am."

Fortunate prophecy! Martha went to live as servant with Governor Wentworth at his mansion at Little Harbor, looking out to sea. Seven years passed, and the "thin slip of a girl," who promised to be no great beauty, had flowered into the loveliest of women, with a lip like a cherry and a cheek like a tea-rose—a lady by instinct, one of Nature's own ladies. The governor, a lonely widower, and not too young, fell in love with his fair handmaid. Without stating his purpose to any one, Governor Wentworth invited a number of friends (among others the Rev. Arthur Brown) to dine with him at Little Harbor on his birthday. After the dinner, which was a very elaborate one, was at an end, and the guests were discussing their tobacco-pipes, Martha Hilton glided into the room, and stood blushing in front of the chimney-place. She was exquisitely dressed, as you may conceive, and wore her hair three stories high. The guests stared at each other, and particularly at her, and wondered. Then the governor, rising from his seat,

"Played slightly with his ruffles, then looked down,
And said unto the Reverend Arthur Brown:
'This is my birthday; it shall likewise be
My wedding-day; and you shall marry me!'"

The rector was dumfounded, knowing the humble footing Martha had held in the house, and could think of nothing cleverer to say than, "To whom, your excellency?" which was not cleaver at all.

"To this lady," replied the governor, taking Martha Hilton by the hand. The Rev. Arthur Brown hesitated. "As the Chief Magistrate of New Hampshire I command you to marry me!" cried the choleric old governor.

And so it was done; and the pretty kitchen-maid became Lady Wentworth, and did ride in her own chariot. She would not have been a woman if she had not taken an early opportunity to drive by Staver's hotel!

Lady Wentworth had a keen appreciation of the dignity of her new station, and became a grand lady at once. A few days after her marriage, dropping her ring on the floor, she languidly ordered her servant to pick it up. The servant, who appears to have had a fair sense of humor, grew suddenly near-sighted, and was unable to the ring until Lady Wentworth stooped and placed her ladyship's finger upon it. She turned out a faultless wife, however; and Governor Wentworth at his death, which occurred in 1770, signified his approval of her by leaving her his entire estate. She married again without changing name, accepting the hand, and what there was of the heart, of Michael Wentworth, a retired colonel of the British army, who came to this country in 1767. Colonel Wentworth (not connected, I think, with the Portsmouth branch of Wentworths) seems to have been of a convivial turn of mind. He shortly dissipated his wife's fortune in high living, and died abruptly in New York—it was supposed by his own hand. His last words—a quite unique contribution to the literature of last words—were, "I have had my cake, and ate it," which showed that the colonel within his own modest limitations was a philosopher.

The seat of Governor Wentworth at Little Harbor—a pleasant walk from Market Square—is well worth a visit. Time and change have laid their hands more lightly on this rambling old pile than on any other of the old homes in Portsmouth. When you cross the threshold of the door you step into the colonial period. Here the Past seems to have halted courteously, waiting for you to catch up with it. Inside and outside the Wentworth mansion remains nearly as the old governor left it; and though it is no longer in the possession of the family, the present owners, in their willingness to gratify the decent curiosity of strangers, show a hospitality which has always characterized the place.

The house is an architectural freak. The main building—if it is the main building—is generally two stories in height, with irregular wings forming three sides of a square which opens in the water. It is, in brief, a cluster of whimsical extensions that look as if they had been built at different periods, which I believe was not the case. The mansion was completed in 1750. It originally contained fifty-two rooms; a portion of the structure was removed about half a century ago, leaving forty-five apartments. The chambers were connected in the oddest manner, by unexpected steps leading up or down, and capricious little passages that seem to have been the unhappy afterthoughts of the architect. But it is a mansion on a grand scale, and with a grand air. The cellar was arranged for the stabling of a troop of thirty horse in times of danger. The council-chamber, where for many years all questions of vital importance to the State were discussed, is a spacious, high-studded room, finished in the richest style of the last century. It is said that the ornamentation of the huge mantel, carved with knife and chisel, cost the workman a year's constant labor. At the entrance to the council-chamber are still the racks for the twelve muskets of the governor's guard—so long ago dismissed!

Some valuable family portraits adorn the walls here, among which is a fine painting-yes, by our friend Copley—of the lovely Dorothy Quincy, who married John Hancock, and afterward became Madam Scott. This lady was a niece of Dr. Holme's "Dorothy Q." Opening on the council-chamber is a large billiard-room; the billiard-table is gone, but an ancient spinnet, with the prim air of an ancient maiden lady, and of a wheezy voice, is there; and in one corner stands a claw-footed buffet, near which the imaginative nostril may still detect a faint and tantalizing odor of colonial punch. Opening also on the council-chamber are several tiny apartments, empty and silent now, in which many a close rubber has been played by illustrious hands. The stillness and loneliness of the old house seem saddest here. The jeweled fingers are dust, the merry laughs have turned themselves into silent, sorrowful phantoms, stealing from chamber to chamber. It is easy to believe in the traditional ghost that haunts the place—

"A jolly place in times of old,
But something ails it now!"

The mansion at Little Harbor is not the only historic house that bears the name of Wentworth. On Pleasant Street, at the head of Washington Street, stands the abode of another colonial worthy, Governor John Wentworth, who held office from 1767 down to the moment when the colonies dropped the British yoke as if it had been the letter H. For the moment the good gentleman's occupation was gone. He was a royalist of the most florid complexion. In 1775, a man named John Fenton, and ex-captain in the British army, who had managed to offend the Sons of Liberty, was given sanctuary in this house by the governor, who refused to deliver the fugitive to the people. The mob planted a small cannon (unloaded) in front of the doorstep and threatened to open fire if Fenton were not forthcoming. He forth-with came. The family vacated the premises via the back-yard, and the mob entered, doing considerable damage. The broken marble chimney-place still remains, mutely protesting against the uncalled-for violence. Shortly after this event the governor made his way to England, where his loyalty was rewarded first with a governorship and then with a pension of L500. He was governor of Nova Scotia from 1792 to 1800, and died in Halifax in 1820. This house is one of the handsomest old dwellings in the town, and promises to outlive many of its newest neighbors. The parlor has undergone no change whatever since the populace rushed into it over a century ago. The furniture and adornments occupy their original positions and the plush on the walls has not been replaced by other hangings. In the hall—deep enough for the traditional duel of baronial romance—are full-length portraits of the several governors and sundry of their kinsfolk.

There is yet a third Wentworth house, also decorated with the shade of a colonial governor—there were three Governors Wentworth—but we shall pass it by, though out of no lack of respect for that high official personage whose commission was signed by Joseph Addison, Esq., Secretary of State under George I.

V
OLD STRAWBERRY BANK

THESE old houses have perhaps detained us too long. They are merely the crumbling shells of things dead and gone, of persons and manners and customs that have left no very distinct record of themselves, excepting here and there in some sallow manuscript which has luckily escaped the withering breath of fire, for the old town, as I have remarked, has managed, from the earliest moment of its existence, to burn itself up periodically. It is only through the scattered memoranda of ancient town clerks, and in the files of worm-eaten and forgotten newspapers, that we are enabled to get glimpses of that life which was once so real and positive and has now become a shadow. I am of course speaking of the early days of the settlement on Strawberry Bank. They were stormy and eventful days. The dense forest which surrounded the clearing was alive with hostile red-men. The sturdy pilgrim went to sleep with his firelock at his bedside, not knowing at what moment he might be awakened by the glare of his burning hayricks and the piercing war-whoops of the Womponoags. Year after year he saw his harvest reaped by a sickle of flames, as he peered through the loop-holes of the blockhouse, whither he had flown in hot haste with goodwife and little ones. The blockhouse at Strawberry Bank appears to have been on an extensive scale, with stockades for the shelter of cattle. It held large supplies of stores, and was amply furnished with arquebuses, sakers, and murtherers, a species of naval ordnance which probably did not belie its name. It also boasted, we are told, of two drums for training-days, and no fewer than fifteen hautboys and soft-voiced recorders—all which suggests a mediaeval castle, or a grim fortress in the time of Queen Elizabeth. To the younger members of the community glass or crockery ware was an unknown substance; to the elders it was a memory. An iron pot was the pot-of-all-work, and their table utensils were of beaten pewter. The diet was also of the simplest—pea-porridge and corn-cake, with a mug of ale or a flagon of Spanish wine, when they could get it.

John Mason, who never resided in this country, but delegated the management of his plantation at Ricataqua and Newichewannock to stewards, died before realizing any appreciable return from his enterprise.

He spared no endeavor meanwhile to further its prosperity. In 1632, three years before his death, Mason sent over from Denmark a number of neat cattle, "of a large breed and yellow colour." The herd thrived, and it is said that some of the stock is still extant on farms in the vicinity of Portsmouth. Those old first families had a kind of staying quality!

In May, 1653, the inhabitants of the settlement petitioned the General Court at Boston to grant them a definite township—for the boundaries were doubtful—and the right to give it a proper name. "Whereas the name of this plantation att present being Strabery Banke, accidentlly soe called, by reason of a banke where strawberries was found in this place, now we humbly desire to have it called Portsmouth, being a name most suitable for this place, it being the river's mouth, and good as any in this land, and your petit'rs shall humbly pray," etc.

Throughout that formative period, and during the intermittent French wars, Portsmouth and the outlying districts were the scenes of bloody Indian massacres. No portion of the New England colony suffered more. Famine, fire, pestilence, and war, each in turn, and sometimes in conjunction, beleaguered the little stronghold, and threatened to wipe it out. But that was not to be.

The settlement flourished and increased in spite of all, and as soon as it had leisure to draw breath, it bethought itself of the school-house and the jail—two incontestable signs of budding civilization. At a town meeting in 1662, it was ordered "that a cage be made or some other meanes invented by the selectmen to punish such as sleepe or take tobacco on the Lord's day out of the meetinge in the time of publique service." This salutary measure was not, for some reason, carried into effect until nine years later, when Captain John Pickering, who seems to have had as many professions as Michelangelo, undertook to construct a cage twelve feet square and seven feet high, with a pillory on top; "the said Pickering to make a good strong dore and make a substantiale payre of stocks and places the same in said cage." A spot conveniently near the west end on the meeting-house was selected as the site for this ingenious device. It is more than probable that "the said Pickering" indirectly furnished an occasional bird for his cage, for in 1672 we find him and one Edward Westwere authorized by the selectmen to "keepe houses of publique entertainment." He was a versatile individual, this John Pickering—soldier, miller, moderator, carpenter, lawyer, and innkeeper. Michelangelo need not blush to be bracketed with him. In the course of a long and variegated career he never failed to act according to his lights, which he always kept well trimmed. That Captain Pickering subsequently became the grandfather, at several removes, of the present writer was no fault of the Captain's, and should not be laid up against him.

Down to 1696, the education of the young appears to have been a rather desultory and tentative matter; "the young idea" seems to have been allowed to "shoot" at whatever it wanted to; but in that year it was voted "that care be taken that an abell scollmaster [skullmaster!] be provided for the towen as the law directs, not visious in conversation." That was perhaps demanding too much; for it was not until "May ye 7" of the following year that the selectmen were fortunate enough to put their finger on this rara avis in the person of Mr. Tho. Phippes, who agreed "to be scollmaster for the the towen this yr insewing for teaching the inhabitants children in such manner as other schollmasters yously doe throughout the countrie: for his soe doinge we the sellectt men in behalfe of ower towen doe ingage to pay him by way of rate twenty pounds and yt he shall and may reserve from every father or master that sends theyer children to school this yeare after ye rate of 16s. for readers, writers and cypherers 20s., Lattiners 24s."

Modern advocates of phonetic spelling need not plume themselves on their originality. The town clerk who wrote that delicious "yously doe" settles the question. It is to be hoped that Mr. Tho. Phippes was not only "not visious in conversation," but was more conventional in his orthography. He evidently gave satisfaction, and clearly exerted an influence on the town clerk, Mr. Samuel Keais, who ever after shows a marked improvement in his own methods. In 1704 the town empowered the selectmen "to call and settell a gramer scoll according to ye best of yower judgement and for ye advantag [Keais is obviously dead now] of ye youth of ower town to learn them to read from ye primer, to wright and sypher and to learne ym the tongues and good-manners." On this occasion it was Mr. William Allen, of Salisbury, who engaged "dilligently to attend ye school for ye present yeare, and tech all childern yt can read in thaire psallters and upward." From such humble beginnings were evolved some of the best public high schools at present in New England.

Portsmouth did not escape the witchcraft delusion, though I believe that no hangings took place within the boundaries of the township. Dwellers by the sea are generally superstitious; sailors always are. There is something in the illimitable expanse of sky and water that dilates the imagination. The folk who live along the coast live on the edge of a perpetual mystery; only a strip of yellow sand or gray rock separates them from the unknown; they hear strange voices in the winds at midnight, they are haunted by the spectres of the mirage. Their minds quickly take the impress of uncanny things. The witches therefore found a sympathetic atmosphere in Newscastle, at the mouth of the Piscataqua—that slender paw of land which reaches out into the ocean and terminates in a spread of sharp, flat rocks, lie the claws of an amorous cat. What happened to the good folk of that picturesque little fishing-hamlet is worth retelling in brief. In order properly to retell it, a contemporary witness shall be called upon to testify in the case of the Stone-Throwing Devils of Newcastle. It is the Rev. Cotton Mather who addresses you—"On June 11, 1682, showers of stones were thrown by an invisible hand upon the house of George Walton at Portsmouth [Newcastle was then a part of the town]. Whereupon the people going out found the gate wrung off the hinges, and stones flying and falling thick about them, and striking of them seemingly with a great force, but really affecting 'em no more than if a soft touch were given them. The glass windows were broken by the stones that came not from without, but from within; and other instruments were in a like manner hurled about. Nine of the stones they took up, whereof some were as hot as if they came out of the fire; and marking them they laid them on the table; but in a little while they found some of them again flying about. The spit was carried up the chimney, and coming down with the point forward, stuck in the back log, from whence one of the company removing it, it was by an invisible hand thrown out at the window. This disturbance continued from day to day; and sometimes a dismal hollow whistling would be heard, and sometimes the trotting and snorting of a horse, but nothing to be seen. The man went up the Great Bay in a boat on to a farm which he had there; but the stones found him out, and carrying from the house to the boat a stirrup iron the iron came jingling after him through the woods as far as his house; and at last went away and was heard no more. The anchor leaped overboard several times and stopt the boat. A cheese was taken out of the press, and crumbled all over the floor; a piece of iron stuck into the wall, and a kettle hung thereon. Several cocks of hay, mow'd near the house, were taken up and hung upon the trees, and others made into small whisps, and scattered about the house. A man was much hurt by some of the stones. He was a Quaker, and suspected that a woman, who charged him with injustice in detaining some land from here, did, by witchcraft, occasion these preternatural occurrences. However, at last they came to an end."

Now I have done with thee, O credulous and sour Cotton Mather! so get thee back again to thy tomb in the old burying-ground on Copp's Hill, where, unless thy nature is radically changed, thou makest it uncomfortable for those about thee.

Nearly a hundred years afterwards, Portsmouth had another witch—a tangible witch in this instance—one Molly Bridget, who cast her malign spell on the eleemosynary pigs at the Almshouse, where she chanced to reside at the moment. The pigs were manifestly bewitched, and Mr. Clement March, the superintendent of the institution, saw only one remedy at hand, and that was to cut off and burn the tips of their tales. But when the tips were cut off they disappeared, and it was in consequence quite impracticable to burn them. Mr. March, who was a gentleman of expedients, ordered that all the chips and underbrush in the yard should be made into heaps and consumed, hoping thus to catch and do away with the mysterious and provoking extremities. The fires were no sooner lighted than Molly Bridget rushed from room to room in a state of frenzy. With the dying flames her own vitality subsided, and she was dead before the ash-piles were cool. I say it seriously when I say that these are facts of which there is authentic proof.

If the woman had recovered, she would have fared badly, even at that late period, had she been in Salem; but the death-penalty has never been hastily inflicted in Portsmouth. The first execution that ever took place there was that of Sarah Simpson and Penelope Kenny, for the murder of an infant in 1739. The sheriff was Thomas Packer, the same official who, twenty-nine years later, won unenviable notoriety at the hanging of Ruth Blay. The circumstances are set forth by the late Albert Laighton in a spirited ballad, which is too long to quote in full. The following stanzas, however, give the pith of the story—

"And a voice among them shouted,
"Pause before the deed is done;
We have asked reprieve and pardon
For the poor misguided one.'

"But these words of Sheriff Packer
Rang above the swelling noise:
'Must I wait and lose my dinner?
Draw away the cart, my boys!'

"Nearer came the sound and louder,
Till a steed with panting breath,
From its sides the white foam dripping,
Halted at the scene of death;

"And a messenger alighted,
Crying to the crowd, 'Make way!
This I bear to Sheriff Packer;
'Tis a pardon for Ruth Blay!'"

But of course he arrived too late—the Law led Mercy about twenty minutes. The crowd dispersed, horror-stricken; but it assembled again that night before the sheriff's domicile and expressed its indignation in groans. His effigy, hanged on a miniature gallows, was afterwards paraded through the streets.

"Be the name of Thomas Packer

A reproach forevermore!"

Laighton's ballad reminds me of that Portsmouth has been prolific in poets, one of whom, at least, has left a mouthful of perennial rhyme for orators—Jonathan Sewell with his

"No pent-up Utica contracts your powers,

But the whole boundless continent is yours."

I have somewhere seen a volume with the alliterative title of "Poets of Portsmouth," in which are embalmed no fewer than sixty immortals!

But to drop into prose again, and have done with this iliad of odds and ends. Portsmouth has the honor, I believe, of establishing the first recorded pauper workhouse—though not in connection with her poets, as might naturally be supposed. The building was completed and tenanted in 1716. Seven years later, an act was passed in England authorizing the establishment of parish workhouses there. The first and only keeper of the Portsmouth almshouse up to 1750 was a woman—Rebecca Austin.

Speaking of first things, we are told by Mr. Nathaniel Adams, in his "Annals of Portsmouth," that on the 20th of April, 1761, Mr. John Stavers began running a stage from that town to Boston. The carriage was a two-horse curricle, wide enough to accommodate three passengers. The fare was thirteen shillings and sixpence sterling per head. The curricle was presently superseded by a series of fat yellow coaches, one of which—nearly a century later, and long after that pleasant mode of travel had fallen obsolete—was the cause of much mental tribulation (1. Some idle reader here and there may possibly recall the burning of the old stage-coach in The Story of a Bad Boy.) to the writer of this chronicle.

The mail and the newspaper are closely associated factors in civilization, so I mention them together, though in this case the newspaper antedated the mail-coach about five years. On October 7, 1756, the first number of "The New Hampshire Gazette and Historical Chronicle" was issued in Portsmouth from the press of Daniel Fowle, who in the previous July had removed from Boston, where he had undergone a brief but uncongenial imprisonment on suspicion of having printed a pamphlet entitled "The Monster of Monsters, by Tom Thumb, Esq.," an essay that contained some uncomplimentary reflections on several official personages. The "Gazette" was the pioneer journal of the province. It was followed at the close of the same year by "The Mercury and Weekly Advertiser," published by a former apprentice of Fowle, a certain Thomas Furber, backed by a number of restless Whigs, who considered the "Gazette" not sufficiently outspoken in the cause of liberty. Mr. Fowle, however, contrived to hold his own until the day of his death. Fowle had for pressman a faithful negro named Primus, a full-blooded African. Whether Primus was a freeman or a slave I am unable to state. He lived to a great age, and was a prominent figure among the people of his own color.

Negro slavery was common in New England at that period. In 1767, Portsmouth numbered in its population a hundred and eighty-eight slaves, male and female. Their bondage, happily, was nearly always of a light sort, if any bondage can be light. They were allowed to have a kind of government of their own; indeed, were encouraged to do so, and no unreasonable restrictions were placed on their social enjoyment. They annually elected a king and counselors, and celebrated the event with a procession. The aristocratic feeling was highly developed in them. The rank of the master was the slave's rank. There was a great deal of ebony standing around on its dignity in those days. For example, Governor Langdon's manservant, Cyrus Bruce, was a person who insisted on his distinction, and it was recognized. His massive gold chain and seals, his cherry-colored small-clothes and silk stockings, his ruffles and silver shoe-buckles, were a tradition long after Cyrus himself was pulverized.

In cases of minor misdemeanor among them, the negros themselves were permitted to be judge and jury. Their administration of justice was often characteristically naive. Mr. Brewster gives an amusing sketch of one of their sessions. King Nero is on the bench, and one Cato—we are nothing if not classical—is the prosecuting attorney. The name of the prisoner and the nature of his offense are not disclosed to posterity. In the midst of the proceedings the hour of noon is clanged from the neighboring belfry of the Old North Church. "The evidence was not gone through with, but the servants could stay no longer from their home duties. They all wanted to see the whipping, but could not conveniently be present again after dinner. Cato ventured to address the King: Please you Honor, best let the fellow have his whipping now, and finish the trial after dinner. The request seemed to be the general wish of the company: so Nero ordered ten lashes, for justice so far as the trial went, and ten more at the close of the trial, should he be found guilty!"

Slavery in New Hampshire was never legally abolished, unless Abraham Lincoln did it. The State itself has not ever pronounced any emancipation edict. During the Revolutionary War the slaves were generally emancipated by their masters. That many of the negros, who had grown gray in service, refused their freedom, and elected to spend the rest of their lives as pensioners in the families of their late owners, is a circumstance that illustrates the kindly ties which held between slave and master in the old colonial days in New England.

The institution was accidental and superficial, and never had any real root in the Granite State. If the Puritans could have found in the Scriptures any direct sanction of slavery, perhaps it would have continued awhile longer, for the Puritan carried his religion into the business affairs of life; he was not even able to keep it out of his bills of lading. I cannot close this rambling chapter more appropriately and solemnly than by quoting from one of those same pious bills of landing. It is dated June, 1726, and reads: "Shipped by the grace of God in good order and well conditioned, by Wm. Pepperills on there own acct. and risque, in and upon the good Briga called the William, whereof is master under God for this present voyage George King, now riding at anchor in the river Piscataqua and by God's grace bound to Barbadoes." Here follows a catalogue of the miscellaneous cargo, rounded off with: "And so God send the good Briga to her desired port in safety. Amen."

VI
SOME OLD PORTSMOUTH PROFILES

I DOUBT if any New England town ever turned out so many eccentric characters as Portsmouth. From 1640 down to about 1848 there must have been something in the air of the place that generated eccentricity. In another chapter I shall explain why the conditions have not been favorable to the development of individual singularity during the latter half of the present century. It is easier to do that than fully to account for the numerous queer human types which have existed from time to time previous to that period.

In recently turning over the pages of Mr. Brewster's entertaining collection of Portsmouth sketches, I have been struck by the number and variety of the odd men and women who appear incidentally on the scene. They are, in the author's intention, secondary figures in the background of his landscape, but they stand very much in the foreground of one's memory after the book is laid aside. One finds one's self thinking quite as often of that squalid old hut-dweller up by Sagamore Creek as of General Washington, who visited the town in 1789. Conservatism and respectability have their values, certainly; but has not the unconventional its values also? If we render unto that old hut-dweller the things which are that old hut-dweller's, we must concede him his picturesqueness. He was dirty, and he was not respectable; but he is picturesque—now that he is dead.

If the reader has five or ten minutes to waste, I invite him to glance at a few old profiles of persons who, however substantial they once were, are now leading a life of mere outlines. I would like to give them a less faded expression, but the past is very chary of yielding up anything more than its shadows.

The first who presents himself is the ruminative hermit already mentioned—a species of uninspired Thoreau. His name was Benjamin Lear. So far as his craziness went, he might have been a lineal descendant of that ancient king of Britain who figures on Shakespeare's page. Family dissensions made a recluse of King Lear; but in the case of Benjamin there were no mitigating circumstances. He had no family to trouble him, and his realm remained undivided. He owned an excellent farm on the south side of Sagamore Creek, a little to the west of the bridge, and might have lived at ease, if personal comfort had not been distasteful to him. Personal comfort entered into no part of Lear's. To be alone filled the little pint-measure of his desire. He ensconced himself in a wretched shanty, and barred the door, figuratively, against all the world. Wealth—what would have been wealth to him—lay within his reach, but he thrust it aside; he disdained luxury as he disdained idleness, and made no compromise with convention. When a man cuts himself absolutely adrift from custom, what an astonishingly light spar floats him! How few his wants are, after all! Lear was of a cheerful disposition, and seems to have been wholly inoffensive—at a distance. He fabricated his own clothes, and subsisted chiefly on milk and potatoes, the product of his realm. He needed nothing but an island to be a Robinson Crusoe. At rare intervals he flitted like a frost-bitten apparition through the main street of Portsmouth, which he always designated as "the Bank," a name that had become obsolete fifty or a hundred years before. Thus, for nearly a quarter of a century, Benjamin Lear stood aloof from human intercourse. In his old age some of the neighbors offered him shelter during the tempestuous winter months; but he would have none of it—he defied wind and weather. There he lay in his dilapidated hovel in his last illness, refusing to allow any one to remain with him overnight—and the mercury four degrees below zero. Lear was born in 1720, and vegetated eighty-two years.

I take it that Timothy Winn, of whom we have only a glimpse, would like to have more, was a person better worth knowing. His name reads like the title of some old-fashioned novel—"Timothy Winn, or the Memoirs of a Bashful Gentleman." He came to Portsmouth from Woburn at the close of the last century, and set up in the old museum-building on Mulberry Street what was called "a piece goods store." He was the third Timothy in his monotonous family, and in order to differentiate himself he inscribed on the sign over his shop door, "Timothy Winn, 3d," and was ever after called "Three-Penny Winn." That he enjoyed the pleasantry, and clung to his sign, goes to show that he was a person who would ripen on further acquaintance, were further acquaintance now practicable. His next-door neighbor, Mr. Leonard Serat, who kept a modest tailoring establishment, also tantalizes us a little with a dim intimation of originality. He plainly was without literary prejudices, for on one face of his swinging sign was painted the word Taylor, and on the other Tailor. This may have been a delicate concession to that part of the community—the greater part, probably—which would have spelled it with a y.

The building in which Messrs. Winn and Serat had their shops was the property of Nicholas Rousselet, a French gentleman of Demerara, the story of whose unconventional courtship of Miss Catherine Moffatt is pretty enough to bear retelling, and entitles him to a place in our limited collection of etchings. M. Rousselet had doubtless already mad excursions into the pays de tendre, and given Miss Catherine previous notice of the state of his heart, but it was not until one day during the hour of service at the Episcopal church that he brought matters to a crisis by handing to Miss Moffatt a small Bible, on the fly-leaf of which he had penciled the fifth verse of the Second Epistle of John—

"And now I beseech thee, lady, not as though I
wrote a new commandment unto thee, but that
which we had from the beginning, that we love one another."

This was not to be resisted, at lease not by Miss Catherine, who demurely handed the volume back to him with a page turned down at the sixteenth verse in the first chapter of Ruth—

"Whither thou goest, I will go; and where thou lodgest, I
will lodge: thy people shall be my people, and thy God my
God: where thou diest, will I die, and there will I be
buried: the Lord do so to me, and more also, if aught but
death part thee and me."

Aside from this quaint touch of romance, what attaches me to the happy pair—for the marriage was a fortunate one—is the fact that the Rousselets made their home in the old Atkinson mansion, which stood directly opposite my grandfather's house on Court Street and was torn down in my childhood, to my great consternation. The building had been unoccupied for a quarter of a century, and was fast falling into decay with all its rich wood-carvings at cornice and lintel; but was it not full of ghosts, and if the old barracks were demolished, would not these ghosts, or some of them at least, take refuge in my grandfather's house just across the way? Where else could they bestow themselves so conveniently? While the ancient mansion was in process of destruction, I used to peep round the corner of our barn at the workmen, and watch the indignant phantoms go soaring upward in spiral clouds of colonial dust.

A lady differing in many ways from Catherine Moffatt was the Mary Atkinson (once an inmate of this same manor house) who fell to the lot of the Rev. William Shurtleff, pastor of the South Church between 1733 and 1747. From the worldly standpoint, it was a fine match for the Newcastle clergyman—beauty, of the eagle-beaked kind; wealth, her share of the family plate; high birth, a sister to the Hon. Theodore Atkinson. But if the exemplary man had cast his eyes lower, peradventure he had found more happiness, though ill-bred persons without family plate are not necessarily amiable. Like Socrates, this long-suffering divine had always with him an object on which to cultivate heavenly patience, and patience, says the Eastern proverb, is the key to content. The spirit of Xantippe seems to have taken possession of Mrs. Shurtleff immediately after her marriage. The freakish disrespect with which she used her meek consort was a heavy cross to bear at a period in New England when clerical dignity was at its highest sensitive point. Her devices for torturing the poor gentleman were inexhaustible. Now she lets his Sabbath ruffs go unstarched; now she scandalizes him by some unseemly and frivolous color in her attire; now she leaves him to cook his own dinner at the kitchen coals; and now she locks him in his study, whither he has retired for a moment or two of prayer, previous to setting forth to perform the morning service. The congregation has assembled; the sexton has tolled the bell twice as long as is custom, and is beginning a third carillon, full of wonder that his reverence does not appear; and there sits Mistress Shurtleff in the family pew with a face as complacent as that of the cat that has eaten the canary. Presently the deacons appeal to her for information touching the good doctor. Mistress Shurtleff sweetly tells them that the good doctor was in his study when she left home. There he is found, indeed, and released from durance, begging the deacons to keep his mortification secret, to "give it an understanding, but no tongue." Such was the discipline undergone by the worthy Dr. Shurtleff on his earthly pilgrimage. A portrait of this patient man—now a saint somewhere—hangs in the rooms of the New England Historical and Genealogical Society in Boston. There he can be seen in surplice and bands, with his lamblike, apostolic face looking down upon the heavy antiquarian labors of his busy descendants.

Whether or not a man is to be classed as eccentric who vanishes without rhyme or reason on his wedding-night is a query left to the reader's decision. We seem to have struck a matrimonial vein, and must work it out. In 1768, Mr. James McDonough was one of the wealthiest men in Portsmouth, and the fortunate suitor for the hand of a daughter of Jacob Sheafe, a town magnate. The home of the bride was decked and lighted for the nuptials, the banquet-table was spread, and the guests were gathered. The minister in his robe stood by the carven mantelpiece, book in hand, and waited. Then followed an awkward interval—there was a hitch somewhere. A strange silence fell upon the laughing groups; the air grew tense with expectation; in the pantry, Amos Boggs, the butler, in his agitation split a bottle of port over his new cinnamon-colored small-clothes. Then a whisper—a whisper suppressed these twenty minutes—ran through the apartments,—"The bridegroom has not come!". He never came. The mystery of that night remains a mystery after the lapse of a century and a quarter.

What had become of James McDonough? The assassination of so notable a person in a community where every strange face was challenged, where every man's antecedents were known, could not have been accomplished without leaving some slight traces. Not a shadow of foul play was discovered. That McDonough had been murdered or had committed suicide were theories accepted at first by a few, and then by no one. On the other hand, he was in love with his fiancee, he had wealth, power, position—why had he fled? He was seen a moment on the public street, and then never seen again. It was as if he turned into air. Meanwhile the bewilderment of the bride was dramatically painful. If McDonough had been waylaid and killed, she could mourn for him. If he had deserted her, she could wrap herself in her pride. But neither course lay open to her, then or afterward. In one of the Twice Told Tales Hawthorne deals with a man named Wakefield, who disappears with like suddenness, and lives unrecognized for twenty years in a street not far from his abandoned hearthside. Such expunging of one's self was not possible in Portsmouth; but I never think of McDonough without recalling Wakefield. I have an inexplicable conviction that for many a year James McDonough, in some snug ambush, studied and analyzed the effect of his own startling disappearance.

Some time in the year 1758, there dawned upon Portsmouth a personage bearing the ponderous title of King's Attorney, and carrying much gold lace about him. This gilded gentleman was Mr. Wyseman Clagett, of Bristol, England, where his father dwelt on the manor of Broad Oaks, in a mansion with twelve chimneys, and kept a coach and eight or ten servants. Up to the moment of his advent in the colonies, Mr. Wyseman Clagett had evidently not been able to keep anything but himself. His wealth consisted of his personal decorations, the golden frogs on his lapels, and the tinsel at his throat; other charms he had none. Yet with these he contrived to dazzle the eyes of Lettice Mitchel, one of the young beauties of the province, and to cause her to forget that she had plighted troth with a Mr. Warner, then in Europe, and destined to return home with a disturbed heart. Mr. Clagett was a man of violent temper and ingenious vindictiveness, and proved more than a sufficient punishment for Lettice's infidelity. The trifling fact that Warner was dead—he died shortly after his return—did not interfere with the course of Mr. Clagett's jealousy; he was haunted by the suspicion that Lettice regretted her first love, having left nothing undone to make her do so. "This is to pay Warner's debts," remarked Mr. Clagett, as he twitched off the table-cloth and wrecked the tea-things.

In his official capacity he was a relentless prosecutor. The noun Clagett speedily turned itself into a verb; "to Clagett" meant "to prosecute;" they were convertible terms. In spite of his industrious severity, and his royal emoluments, if such existed, the exchequer of the King's Attorney showed a perpetual deficit. The stratagems to which he resorted from time to time in order to raise unimportant sums reminded one of certain scenes in Moliere's comedies.

Mr. Clagett had for his ame damnee a constable of the town. They were made for each other; they were two flowers with but a single stem, and this was their method of procedure: Mr. Clagett dispatched one of his servants to pick a quarrel with some countryman on the street, or some sailor drinking at an inn: the constable arrested the sailor or the countryman, as the case might be, and hauled the culprit before Mr. Clagett; Mr. Clagett read the culprit a moral lesson, and fined him five dollars and costs. The plunder was then divided between the conspirators—two hearts that beat as one—Clagett, of course, getting the lion's share. Justice was never administered in a simpler manner in any country. This eminent legal light was extinguished in 1784, and the wick laid away in the little churchyard in Litchfield, New Hampshire. It is a satisfaction, even after such a lapse of time, to know that Lettice survived the King's Attorney sufficiently long to be very happy with somebody else. Lettice Mitchel was scarcely eighteen when she married Wyseman Clagett.

About eighty years ago, a witless fellow named Tilton seems to have been a familiar figure on the streets of the old town. Mr. Brewster speaks of him as "the well-known idiot, Johnny Tilton," as if one should say, "the well-known statesman, Daniel Webster." It is curious to observe how any sort of individuality gets magnified in this parochial atmosphere, where everything lacks perspective, and nothing is trivial. Johnny Tilton does not appear to have had much individuality to start with; it was only after his head was cracked that he showed any shrewdness whatever. That happened early in his unobtrusive boyhood. He had frequently watched the hens flying out of the loft window in his father's stable, which stood in the rear of the Old Bell Tavern. It occurred to Johnny, one day, that though he might not be as bright as other lads, he certainly was in no respect inferior to a hen. So he placed himself on the sill of the window in the loft, flapped his arms, and took flight. The New England Icarus alighted head downward, lay insensible for a while, and was henceforth looked upon as a mortal who had lost his wits. Yet at odd moments his cloudiness was illumined by a gleam of intelligence such as had not been detected in him previous to his mischance. As Polonius said of Hamlet—another unstrung mortal—Tilton's replies had "a happiness that often madness hits on, which reason and sanity could not so prosperously be delivered of." One morning, he appeared at the flour-mill with a sack of corn to be ground for the almshouse, and was asked what he knew. "Some things I know," replied poor Tilton, "and some things I don't know. I know the miller's hogs grow fat, but I don't know whose corn they fat on." To borrow another word from Polonius, though this be madness, yet there was method in it. Tilton finally brought up in the almshouse, where he was allowed the liberty of roaming at will through the town. He loved the water-side as if he had had all his senses. Often he was seen to stand for hours with a sunny, torpid smile on his lips, gazing out upon the river where its azure ruffles itself into silver against the islands. He always wore stuck in his hat a few hen's feathers, perhaps with some vague idea of still associating himself with the birds of the air, if hens can come into that category.

George Jaffrey, third of the name, was a character of another complexion, a gentleman born, a graduate of Harvard in 1730, and one of His Majesty's Council in 1766—a man with the blood of the lion and the unicorn in every vein. He remained to the bitter end, and beyond, a devout royalist, prizing his shoe-buckles, not because they were of chased silver, but because they bore the tower mark and crown stamp. He stoutly objected to oral prayer, on the ground that it gave rogues and hypocrites an opportunity to impose on honest folk. He was punctilious in his attendance at church, and unfailing in his responses, though not of a particularly devotional temperament. On one occasion, at least, his sincerity is not to be questioned. He had been deeply irritated by some encroachments on the boundaries of certain estates, and had gone to church that forenoon with his mind full of the matter. When the minister in the course of reading the service came to the apostrophe, "Cursed be he who removeth his neighbor's landmark," Mr. Jeffrey's feelings were too many for him, and he cried out "Amen!" in a tone of voice that brought smiles to the adjoining pews.

Mr. Jaffrey's last will and testament was a whimsical document, in spite of the Hon. Jeremiah Mason, who drew up the paper. It had originally been Mr. Jaffrey's plan to leave his possessions to his beloved friend, Colonel Joshua Wentworth; but the colonel by some maladroitness managed to turn the current of Pactolus in another direction. The vast property was bequeathed to George Jaffrey Jeffries, the testator's grandnephew, on condition that the heir, then a lad of thirteen, should drop the name of Jeffries, reside permanently in Portsmouth, and adopt no profession excepting that of gentleman. There is an immense amount of Portsmouth as well as George Jaffrey in that final clause. George the fourth handsomely complied with the requirements, and dying at the age of sixty-six, without issue or assets, was the last of that particular line of Georges. I say that he handsomely complied with the requirements of the will; but my statement appears to be subject to qualification, for on the day of his obsequies it was remarked of him by a caustic contemporary: "Well, yes, Mr. Jaffrey was a gentleman by profession, but not eminent in his profession."

This modest exhibition of profiles, in which I have attempted to preserve no chronological sequence, ends with the silhouette of Dr. Joseph Moses.

If Boston in the colonial days had her Mather Byles, Portsmouth had her Dr. Joseph Moses. In their quality as humorists, the outlines of both these gentlemen have become rather broken and indistinct. "A jest's prosperity lies in the ear that hears it." Decanted wit inevitably loses its bouquet. A clever repartee belongs to the precious moment in which it is broached, and is of a vintage that does not usually bear transportation. Dr. Moses—he received his diploma not from the College of Physicians, but from the circumstance of his having once drugged his private demijohn of rum, and so nailed an inquisitive negro named Sambo—Dr. Moses, as he was always called, had been handed down to us by tradition as a fellow of infinite jest and of most excellent fancy; but I must confess that I find his high spirits very much evaporated. His humor expended itself, for the greater part, in practical pleasantries—like that practiced on the minion Sambo—but these diversions, however facetious to the parties concerned, lack magnetism for outsiders. I discover nothing about him so amusing as the fact that he lived in a tan-colored little tenement, which was neither clapboarded nor shingled, and finally got an epidermis from the discarded shingles of the Old South Church when the roof of that edifice was repaired.

Dr. Moses, like many persons of his time and class, was a man of protean employment—joiner, barber, and what not. No doubt he had much pithy and fluent conversation, all of which escapes us. He certainly impressed the Hon. Theodore Atkinson as a person of uncommon parts, for the Honorable Secretary of the Province, like a second Haroun Al Raschid, often summoned the barber to entertain him with his company. One evening—and this is the only reproducible instance of the doctor's readiness—Mr. Atkinson regaled his guest with a diminutive glass of choice Madeira. The doctor regarded it against the light with the half-closed eye of the connoisseur, and after sipping the molten topaz with satisfaction, inquired how old it was. "Of the vintage of about sixty years ago," was the answer. "Well," said the doctor reflectively, "I never in my life saw so small a thing of such an age." There are other mots of his on record, but their faces are suspiciously familiar. In fact, all the witty things were said aeons ago. If one nowadays perpetrates an original joke, one immediately afterward finds it in the Sanskirt. I am afraid that Dr. Joseph Moses has no very solid claims on us. I have given him place here because he has long had the reputation of a wit, which is almost as good as to be one.

VII
PERSONAL REMINISCENCES

THE running of the first train over the Eastern Road from Boston to Portsmouth—it took place somewhat more than forty years ago—was attended by a serious accident. The accident occurred in the crowded station at the Portsmouth terminus, and was unobserved at the time. The catastrophe was followed, though not immediately, by death, and that also, curiously enough, was unobserved. Nevertheless, this initial train, freighted with so many hopes and the Directors of the Road, ran over and killed—LOCAL CHARACTER.

Up to that day Portsmouth had been a very secluded little community, and had had the courage of its seclusion. From time to time it had calmly produced an individual built on plans and specifications of its own, without regard to the prejudices and conventionalities of outlying districts. This individual was purely indigenous. He was born in the town, he lived to a good old age in the town, and never went out of the place, until he was finally laid under it. To him, Boston, though only fifty-six miles away, was virtually an unknown quantity—only fifty-six miles by brutal geographical measurement, but thousands of miles distant in effect. In those days, in order to reach Boston you were obliged to take a great yellow, clumsy stage-coach, resembling a three-story mud-turtle—if zoologist will, for the sake of the simile, tolerate so daring an invention; you were obliged to take it very early in the morning, you dined at noon at Ipswich, and clattered into the great city with the golden dome just as the twilight was falling, provided always the coach had not shed a wheel by the roadside or one of the leaders had not gone lame. To many worthy and well-to-do persons in Portsmouth, this journey was an event which occurred only twice or thrice during life. To the typical individual with whom I am for the moment dealing, it never occurred at all. The town was his entire world; he was a parochial as a Parisian; Market Street was his Boulevard des Italiens, and the North End his Bois de Boulogne.

Of course there were varieties of local characters without his limitations; venerable merchants retired from the East India trade; elderly gentlewomen, with family jewels and personal peculiarities; one or two scholarly recluses in by-gone cut of coat, haunting the Athenaeum reading-room; ex-sea captains, with rings on their fingers, like Simon Danz's visitors in Longfellow's poem—men who had played busy parts in the bustling world, and had drifted back to Old Strawberry Bank in the tranquil sunset of their careers. I may say, in passing, that these ancient mariners, after battling with terrific hurricanes and typhoons on every known sea, not infrequently drowned themselves in pleasant weather in small sail-boats on the Piscataqua River. Old sea-dogs who had commanded ships of four or five hundred tons had naturally slight respect for the potentialities of sail-boats twelve feet long. But there was to be no further increase of these odd sticks—if I may call them so, in no irreverent mood—after those innocent-looking parallel bars indissolubly linked Portsmouth with the capital of the Commonwealth of Massachusetts. All the conditions were to be changed, the old angles to be pared off, new horizons to be regarded. The individual, as an eccentric individual, was to undergo great modifications. If he were not to become extinct—a thing little likely—he was at least to lose his prominence.

However, as I said, local character, in the sense in which the term is here used, was not instantly killed; it died a lingering death, and passed away so peacefully and silently as not to attract general, or perhaps any, notice. This period of gradual dissolution fell during my boyhood. The last of the cocked hats had gone out, and the railway had come in, long before my time; but certain bits of color, certain half obsolete customs and scraps of the past, were still left over. I was not too late, for example, to catch the last town crier—one Nicholas Newman, whom I used to contemplate with awe, and now recall with a sort of affection.

Nicholas Newman—Nicholas was a sobriquet, his real name being Edward—was a most estimable person, very short, cross-eyed, somewhat bow-legged, and with a bell out of all proportion to his stature. I have never since seen a bell of that size disconnected with a church steeple. The only thing about him that matched the instrument of his office was his voice. His "Hear All!" still deafens memory's ear. I remember that he had a queer way of sidling up to one, as if nature in shaping him had originally intended a crab, but thought better of it, and made a town-crier. Of the crustacean intention only a moist thumb remained, which served Mr. Newman in good stead in the delivery of the Boston evening papers, for he was incidentally newsdealer. His authentic duties were to cry auctions, funerals, mislaid children, traveling theatricals, public meetings, and articles lost or found. He was especially strong in announcing the loss of reticules, usually the property of elderly maiden ladies. The unction with which he detailed the several contents, when fully confided to him, would have seemed satirical in another person, but on his part was pure conscientiousness. He would not let so much as a thimble, or a piece of wax, or a portable tooth, or any amiable vanity in the way of tonsorial device, escape him. I have heard Mr. Newman spoken of as "that horrid man." He was a picturesque figure.

Possibly it is because of his bell that I connect the town crier with those dolorous sounds which I used to hear rolling out of the steeple of the Old North every night at nine o'clock—the vocal remains of the colonial curfew. Nicholas Newman has passed on, perhaps crying his losses elsewhere, but this nightly tolling is still a custom. I can more satisfactorily explain why I associate with it a vastly different personality, that of Sol Holmes, the barber, for every night at nine o'clock his little shop on Congress Street was in full blast. Many a time at that hour I have flattened my nose on his window-glass. It was a gay little shop (he called it "an Emporium"), as barber shops generally are, decorated with circus bills, tinted prints, and gaudy fly-catchers of tissue and gold paper. Sol Holmes—whose antecedents to us boys were wrapped in thrilling mystery, we imagined him to have been a prince in his native land—was a colored man, not too dark "for human nature's daily food," and enjoyed marked distinction as one of the few exotics in town. At this juncture the foreign element was at its minimum; every official, from selectman down to the Dogberry of the watch, bore a name that had been familiar to the town for a hundred years or so. The situation is greatly changed. I expect to live to see a Chinese policeman, with a sandal-wood club and a rice-paper pocket handkerchief, patrolling Congress Street.

Holmes was a handsome man, six feet or more in height, and as straight as a pine. He possessed his race's sweet temper, simplicity, and vanity. His martial bearing was a positive factor in the effectiveness of the Portsmouth Greys, whenever those bloodless warriors paraded. As he brought up the rear of the last platoon, with his infantry cap stuck jauntily on the left side of his head and a bright silver cup slung on a belt at his hip, he seemed to youthful eyes one of the most imposing things in the display. To himself he was pretty much "all the company." He used to say, with a drollness which did not strike me until years afterwards, "Boys, I and Cap'n Towle is goin' to trot out 'the Greys' to-morroh." Though strictly honest in all business dealings, his tropical imagination, whenever he strayed into the fenceless fields of autobiography, left much to be desired in the way of accuracy. Compared with Sol Holmes on such occasions, Ananias was a person of morbid integrity. Sol Holmes's tragic end was in singular contrast with his sunny temperament. One night, long ago, he threw himself from the deck of a Sound steamer, somewhere between Stonington and New York. What led or drove him to the act never transpired.

There are few men who were boys in Portsmouth at the period of which I write but will remember Wibird Penhallow and his sky-blue wheelbarrow. I find it difficult to describe him other than vaguely, possibly because Wilbird had no expression whatever in his countenance. With his vacant white face lifted to the clouds, seemingly oblivious of everything, yet going with a sort of heaven-given instinct straight to his destination, he trundled that rattling wheelbarrow for many a year over Portsmouth cobblestones. He was so unconscious of his environment that sometimes a small boy would pop into the empty wheelbarrow and secure a ride without Wibird arriving at any very clear knowledge of the fact. His employment in life was to deliver groceries and other merchandise to purchasers. This he did in a dreamy, impersonal kind of way. It was as if a spirit had somehow go hold of an earthly wheelbarrow and was trundling it quite unconsciously, with no sense of responsibility. One day he appeared at a kitchen door with a two-gallon molasses jug, the top of which was wanting. It was not longer a jug, but a tureen. When the recipient of the damaged article remonstrated with "Goodness gracious, Wibird! You have broken the jug," his features lighted up, and he seemed immensely relieved. "I thought," He remarked, "I heerd somethink crack!"

Wibird Penhallow's heaviest patron was the keeper of a variety store, and the first specimen of a pessimist I ever encountered. He was an excellent specimen. He took exception to everything. He objected to the telegraph, to the railway, to steam in all its applications. Some of his arguments, I recollect, made a deep impression on my mind. "Nowadays," he once observed to me, "if your son or your grandfather drops dead at the other end of creation, you know of it in ten minutes. What's the use? Unless you are anxious to know he's dead, you've got just two or three weeks more to be miserable in." He scorned the whole business, and was faithful to his scorn. When he received a telegram, which was rare, he made a point of keeping it awhile unopened. Through the exercise of this whim he once missed an opportunity of buying certain goods to great advantage. "There!" he exclaimed, "if the telegraph hadn't been invented the idiot would have written to me, and I'd have sent a letter by return coach, and got the goods before he found out prices had gone up in Chicago. If that boy brings me another of those tapeworm telegraphs, I'll throw an axe-handle at him." His pessimism extended up, or down, to generally recognized canons of orthography. They were all iniquitous. If k-n-i-f-e spelled knife, then, he contended, k-n-i-f-e-s was the plural. Diverting tags, written by his own hand in conformity with this theory, were always attached to articles in his shop window. He is long since ded, as he himself would have put it, but his phonetic theory appears to have survived him in crankish brains here and there. As my discouraging old friend was not exactly a public character, like the town crier or Wibird Penhallow, I have intentionally thrown a veil over his identity. I have, so to speak, dropped into his pouch a grain or two of that magical fern-seed which was supposed by our English ancestors, in Elizabeth's reign, to possess the quality of rendering a man invisible.

Another person who singularly interested me at this epoch was a person with whom I had never exchanged a word, whose voice I had never heard, but whose face was as familiar to me as every day could make it. For each morning as I went to school, and each afternoon as I returned, I saw this face peering out of a window in the second story of a shambling yellow house situated in Washington Street, not far from the corner of State. Whether some malign disease had fixed him to the chair he sat on, or whether he had lost the use of his legs, or, possible, had none (the upper part of him was that of a man in admirable health), presented a problem which, with that curious insouciance of youth I made no attempt to solve. It was an established fact, however, that he never went out of that house. I cannot vouch so confidently for the cobwebby legend which wove itself about him. It was to this effect: He had formerly been the master of a large merchantman running between New York and Calcutta; while still in his prime he had abruptly retired from the quarter-deck, and seated himself at that window—where the outlook must have been the reverse of exhilarating, for not ten persons passed in the course of the day, and the hurried jingle of the bells on Parry's bakery-cart was the only sound that ever shattered the silence. Whether it was an amatory or a financial disappointment that turned him into a hermit was left to ingenious conjecture. But there he sat, year in and year out, with his cheek so close to the window that the nearest pane became permanently blurred with his breath; for after his demise the blurr remained.

In this Arcadian era it was possible, in provincial places, for an undertaker to assume the dimensions of a personage. There was a sexton in Portsmouth—his name escapes me, but his attributes do not—whose impressiveness made him own brother to the massive architecture of the Stone Church. On every solemn occasion he was the striking figure, even to the eclipsing of the involuntary object of the ceremony. His occasions, happily, were not exclusively solemn; he added to his other public services that of furnishing ice-cream for the evening parties. I always thought—perhaps it was the working of an unchastened imagination—that he managed to throw into his ice-creams a peculiar chill not attained by either Dunyon or Peduzzi—arcades ambo—the rival confectioners.

Perhaps I should not say rival, for Mr. Dunyon kept a species of restaurant, while Mr. Peduzzi restricted himself to preparing confections to be discussed elsewhere than on his premises. Both gentlemen achieved great popularity in their respective lines, but neither offered to the juvenile population quite the charm of those prim, white-capped old ladies who presided over certain snuffy little shops, occurring unexpectedly in silent side-streets where the football of commerce seemed an incongruous thing. These shops were never intended in nature. They had an impromptu and abnormal air about them. I do not recall one that was not located in a private residence, and was not evidently the despairing expedient of some pathetic financial crisis, similar to that which overtook Miss Hepzibah Pyrcheon in The House of the Seven Gables. The horizontally divided street door—the upper section left open in summer—ushered you, with a sudden jangle of bell that turned your heart over, into a strictly private hall, haunted by the delayed aroma of thousands of family dinners. Thence, through another door, you passed into what had formerly been the front parlor, but was now a shop, with a narrow, brown, wooden counter, and several rows of little drawers built up against the picture-papered wall behind it. Through much use the paint on these drawers was worn off in circles round the polished brass knobs. Here was stored almost every small article required by humanity, from an inflamed emery cushion to a peppermint Gibraltar—the latter a kind of adamantine confectionery which, when I reflect upon it, raises in me the wonder that any Portsmouth boy or girl ever reached the age of fifteen with a single tooth left unbroken. The proprietors of these little knick-knack establishments were the nicest creatures, somehow suggesting venerable doves. They were always aged ladies, sometimes spinsters, sometimes relicts of daring mariners, beached long before. They always wore crisp muslin caps and steel-rimmed spectacles; they were not always amiable, and no wonder, for even doves may have their rheumatism; but such as they were, they were cherished in young hearts, and are, I take it, impossible to-day.

When I look back to Portsmouth as I knew it, it occurs to me that it must have been in some respects unique among New England towns. There were, for instance, no really poor persons in the place; every one had some sufficient calling or an income to render it unnecessary; vagrants and paupers were instantly snapped up and provided for at "the Farm." There was, however, in a gambrel-roofed house here and there, a decayed old gentlewoman, occupying a scrupulously neat room with just a suspicion of maccaboy snuff in the air, who had her meals sent in to her by the neighborhood—as a matter of course, and involving no sense of dependency on her side. It is wonderful what an extension of vitality is given to an old gentlewoman in this condition!

I would like to write about several of those ancient Dames, as they were affectionately called, and to materialize others of the shadows that stir in my recollection; but this would be to go outside the lines of my purpose, which is simply to indicate one of the various sorts of changes that have come over the vie intime of formerly secluded places like Portsmouth—the obliteration of odd personalities, or, if not the obliteration, the general disregard of them. Everywhere in New England the impress of the past is fading out. The few old-fashioned men and women—quaint, shrewd, and racy of the soil—who linger in little, silvery-gray old homesteads strung along the New England roads and by-ways will shortly cease to exist as a class, save in the record of some such charming chronicler as Sarah Jewett, or Mary Wilkins, on whose sympathetic page they have already taken to themselves a remote air, an atmosphere of long-kept lavender and pennyroyal.

Peculiarity in any kind requires encouragement in order to reach flower. The increased facilities of communication between points once isolated, the interchange of customs and modes of thought, make this encouragement more and more difficult each decade. The naturally inclined eccentric finds his sharp outlines rubbed off by unavoidable attrition with a larger world than owns him. Insensibly he lends himself to the shaping hand of new ideas. He gets his reversible cuffs and paper collars from Cambridge, Massachusetts, the scarabaeus in his scarf-pin from Mexico, and his ulster from everywhere. He has passed out of the chrysalis state of Odd Stick; he has ceased to be parochial; he is no longer distinct; he is simply the Average Man.

INDEX OF NAMES

DUNYON, WILLIAM

ELIZABETH, QUEEN

FENTON, JOHN

FOWLE, DANIEL

FOWLE, PRIMUS

FRANKLIN, BENJAMIN

FURBER, THOMAS

GEORGE I

GERRY, ELBRIDGE

GORGES, SIR FERDINAND

GUAST, PIERRE DE

HAM, SUPPLY

HANCOCK, JOHN

HAWTHORNE, NATHANIEL

HILTON, MARTHA

HOLMES, OLIVER WENDELL

HOLMES, SOL

JAFFREY, GEORGE

JAFFRIES, GEORGE JAFFREY

JEWETT, SARAH ORNE

KEAIS, SAMUAL

KEKUANAOA

KENNY, PENELOPE

KNOX, GENERAL HENRY

LAFAYETTE, MARQUIS DE

LAIGHTON, ALBERT

LAIGHTON, OSCAR

LANGDON, COLONEL JOHN

LEAR, BENJAMIN

LONGFELLOW, HENRY WADSWORTH

MACPHEADRIS, ARCHIBALD

MCDONOUGH, JAMES

MASON, JEREMIAH

MASON, JOHN

MASON, JOHN TUFTON

MARCH, CLEMENT

MATHER, REV. COTTON

MESERVE, GEORGE

MICHELANGELO

MITCHEL, LETTUCE

MOFFATT, CATHERINE

MOLIERE

MONTPENSIER, DUC DE

MOSES, JOSEPH

NEWMAN, EDWARD

NOBLE, MARK

ODIORNE, EBEN L.

PACKER, THOMAS

PEDUZZI, DOMINIC

PENHALLOW, WIBIRD

PEPPERELL, SIR WILLIAM

PEPYS, SAMUAL

PHILIPPE, LOUIS

PHIPPES, THOMAS

PHIPPS, GOVERNOR

PICKERING, JOHN

PITT, WILLIAM

POTTLE, WILLIAM

PRING, MARTIN

QUINCY, DOROTHY

ROCHAMBEAU, COUNT DE

ROUSSELET, NICHOLAS

RUTLEDGE, EDWARD

SERAT, LEONARD

SEWELL, JONATHAN

SHAKESPEARE

SHEAFE, JACOB

SHERBURNE, HENRY

SHURTLEFF, MARY ATKINSON

SHURTLEFF, REV. WILLIAM

SIMPSON, SARAH

SMITH, CAPTAIN JOHN

SOCRATES

STAVERS, DAME

STAVERS, JOHN

STEDMAN, EDMUND CLARENCE

STOODLEY, JAMES

THAXTER, CELIA

THOREAU, HENRY DAVID

TILTON, JOHNNY

TOWLE, GEORGE WILLIAM

WALTON, GEORGE

WARNER, JONATHAN

WASHINGTON, GEORGE

WEBSTER, DANIEL

WENTWORTH, BENNING

WENTWORTH, JOHN

WENTWORTH, JOHN 2D

WENTWORTH, COLONEL JOSHUA

WENTWORTH, MARY

WENTWORTH, MICHAEL

WENTWORTH, SARAH

WESTWERE, EDWARD

WHITTIER, JOHN GREENLEAF

WIBIRD, RICHARD

WILKINS, MARY E.

WINN, TIMOTHY

WITHER, GEORGE

XANTIPPE